Spirit Guides

A Beginner's Guide to Communicating with Spirit Guides and Guardian Angels

Table of Contents

Introduction

Do you ever feel like you are fighting a losing battle against life, and you are completely alone? These types of feelings can be destructive and damaging. But what if you knew that the universe and the spiritual world have a team of guides ready to help you, guide you, and protect you from the moment you are born? Even if you don't feel particularly spiritual or in sync with the universe, they are there, waiting for you to reach out and receive their messages.

Maybe you have already been blessed by spiritual messaging. Seemingly normal communications are often sent to give you a nudge in the right direction. Have you ever experienced a "coincidence" that turned up at just the right time?

In this book, we will discuss who these members of your spiritual team are, why they are there, and how you can begin to communicate with them. The spirits don't care what your religious beliefs are; they are simply there for you. Once you know how to interpret their signs, ask them for help, and communicate openly with them, you will be able to use them to their fullest potential to enhance your time here on Earth.

Chapter 1: What are Spirit Guides?

The existence of spirit guides can't be dismissed offhand, because truly, everyone has had an experience where outside forces have influenced them. The difference is that believers will recognize that the spirits and the universe are sending signals and messages while non-believers will pass off the experiences as coincidences and natural life events.

If you believe in spirit guides, then you recognize that they are a shared human experience. They don't just appear to people who believe in them; they are forces that exist purely to assist spiritual growth and lead us on a path of clarity, joy, and inner peace. So, even if the thought of spirit guides as tangible beings may not appeal to your beliefs, you must at least recognize that there are archetypal forms of energy that govern how we live.

In Western spiritual teachings, many forms of spirit guides form a team of mentors to protect incarnated humans and provide them with the knowledge and support they need. Spirit guide is a general term that covers many forms of protectors, including the examples listed below. This list is not exhaustive as some people find that their connections are unique and don't fall into regular groups.

Who Is on Your Team?

First, you will have a major guide, also known as a guardian angel, who is assigned to you before you are born. We will cover guardian angels in more detail later in the book, but for now we will call this major guide your "life guide", and begin with them.

> • **Life guide:** These guardians are with you from the moment you are born to the moment you die and beyond. They chose you because they recognize your spirit as one that resonates with their own. They are the only spirits that never leave your side.
>
> Once you connect with your life geode, you will have a sense of their individuality. You will have a name that you can use to summon them and an overall feeling of their appearance and their background as a spirit. They will connect with you whenever you need them, and they will act as a chaperone for the rest of your spiritual team. Life guides are like office managers who are trained to cut down the chaos.
>
> • **Divine timing guides:** These are the timekeepers of the spiritual world. They have a blueprint for your life and will give you nudges when you need to take certain paths. They are always working to make your life run

smoothly, but that doesn't necessarily mean you will get everything you want.

If you receive messages via numbers and synchronicity, these are the spirits that sent them. Make sure you understand the relevance and symbolism the numbers represent so you can interpret their messages.

• **Warrior guides:** These are incredibly enlightened beings who are there to protect you from all forms of attacks. This can be spiritual, physical, or mental attacks but will focus mainly on psychic matters. These guides are responsible for that troubling gut feeling when you feel something isn't right.

• **Creative guides:** These spirits are responsible for creative matters. They will teach your soul to appreciate the skills and abilities you have and put them to good use. Even the most uncreative soul will benefit from these guides. They will give you alternate creative solutions to all your dilemmas.

• **Gatekeepers:** These are your secondary bodyguard who works closely with your warrior protectors. They hold your Akashic record, a psychic record of every thought and event that has happened in your past, present, and future. This enables them to protect you from all negative energies that threaten to invade your life. Your gatekeeper spirit is like a high-class doorman at an exclusive club with a list. They will only allow entry to the higher forms of energy, and they will block all the negativity.

• **Light beings:** Everyone has times when they despair. The death of loved ones or traumatic events happen to us all. Light beings will be there for you to raise your spirits and help you get through the darkness. They are named light beings because they will literally bring light into your life.

• **Half man half beast:** Also referred to as trans-species, these spirits have embraced human and animal qualities. Many deities have such a form, including Anubis, the jackal-headed god from ancient Egyptian times. Other forms of trans species are mermaids, harpies, and centaurs. The spirits take this form to appear magical and less threatening to people who are hesitant of the spirit world.

• **Ancestor guides:** When members of your family pass away, they are given the opportunity to act as a guide for you. They will also have their own ancestral guides who will join your spiritual team even though generations separate you. If you connect with a spirit, which feels familiar, it could be an ancestral bond. If you feel a connection with this type of spirit, try researching your family tree to discover who it might be and what qualities they bring to the table.

• **Ascended masters:** These are higher beings who have lived fruitful lives and achieved higher spiritual planes. They have been through their own spiritual awakenings and have transcended the cycle of reincarnation and spiritual growth. Now they have a different role to fulfil. The ascended masters will strive to help all of humanity whenever they are facing karmic blockages, or they need the wisdom and counseling from these ultimate teachers.

Popular Ascended Masters You Can Call On

1) **Amitabha:** The ultimate Buddhist comprehensive symbol of love. He lives in paradise yet is never too busy to bring his loving essence into your spiritual world.

2) **Jesus Christ:** The Son of God, Jesus is the embodiment of wisdom and unconditional love. His time on Earth brought him a deeper understanding of the human psyche and the way men and women

work. Call on him for energies of devotion and forgiveness when you need to.

3) **Krishna:** This Hindu deity is the god of compassion and tenderness. He will come to your aid when your spirit is battered and broken to provide a psychic salve. His name is associated with the color blue, and the appearance of this hue will signal when Krishna is visiting you or sending you a message.

4) **Kuthumi:** As one of the masters of ancient wisdom, he oversees the development of humanity. Call on him to advise you on how to achieve higher spiritual goals.

5) **Saint Francis of Assisi:** If you have a particular affinity to animals, you will find a connection to this ascended master. He is a strong spiritual representation of the natural world and helping the environment.

Healing guides: These spirits will come to your aid when you need to heal. This applies to physical traumas as well as spiritual ones. They have been successful healers during their time on Earth and their different incarnations. Think of it as a calling to a particular career; once a healer, always a healer. In the past, they may have been shamanic healers, reiki masters, or traditional healing professionals.

Dragons: You call upon this ultimate force of nature when you need primordial strength. The dragon is the master of the Earth, air, and fire, and he brings all these elements to play. It will come to your aid when you need to change. This could mean you need its help to get rid of elements of your life, or it could be as simple as a change in career.

Gods and goddesses: Deities are never too busy or aloof to help humans. Choose the deity with the strengths you need and ask for their spirit to come into your life.

Some of the Most Powerful Spirit Guides Who are Deities

1) Thor: The ultimate god of thunder, Thor is a righteous spirit who rides the storms on a chariot pulled by goats. If you want to feel it, his power stands beneath an oak tree during a summer storm and looks to the heavens. You will see Thor and his mighty hammer striking fear into the hearts of his enemies. Ask for his strength and power when times are tough.

2) Sol: The Nordic goddess of the sun is a spirit that brings light to your life. Her legend is she rides the golden chariot across the sky chased by wolves. Her strength and light will repair even the most wounded soul.

3) Brigid: This Celtic goddess has three representations that appeal to feminine energies. She is a Mother, a maiden, and a crone, so women of all ages will find her available to them. She has a fiery nature and will provide you with inspiration and hope.

4) Ostara: Goddess of spring and new beginnings. When you are ready to begin your next stage of spiritual development, she will guide you and give you protection. She is also the goddess of fertility, so call on her for help when you need abundance in your life.

5) Bran the blessed: English and Welsh paganism tell the tale of Bran and his mighty strength. Bran embodies the spirit of strength and lack of fear. He was also a historical scribe who recorded the events of his time. He is represented by the crow and will appear in this form if you need his help to bring diplomacy to arguments.

6) Hermes Trismegistus: This spirit is one of the most powerful available to bring knowledge to your world. He originated in Greece, and his followers believed in his doctrines; they made him a God. He then traveled to Egypt to teach his principles there, and they too made him a God. On his return to Greece, he was declared a thrice God. Call on him to discover ways to interconnect with your fellow humans on all planes. He will guide you to a fuller life and enhanced connections to your fellow man.

7) Freya: Also known as Frigg or Freyja, this Nordic goddess will bring love, beauty, and fertility to your life. She is the keeper of the souls of warriors who enter Valhalla for the final time. It is said that once Freya claims a warrior's soul, his time on Earth is over. He is destined to reside in the halls of the gods and enjoy eternal paradise. Freya will come to your aid if you are ready to embrace a different life and feel peace.

8) Tyr: The god of war is ready to help when all else fails. If you have tried to settle disputes with diplomacy and tact and that hasn't worked, call on Tyr for his strength. He is a spirit who will help you stand up for what is right and defeat those who are trying to stop you. He sacrificed his right arm to the wolf Fenrir as a sign of good faith to stop tyranny in his physical life. Think of Tyr as your divine spiritual jurist. He will fight for justice and be your defender and warrior.

9) Athena: The Greek goddess of wisdom is available when you need protection and advice. She is the epitome of urbanization and civilizations, so she will bring order when it is needed.

10) The Green Man: A legendary figure in Celtic religions, he is usually depicted in statues as a symbol of rebirth and spring. His worshippers believe he is the image that represents nature, and that he can help you reconnect to your roots.

Chapter 2: How to Connect with the Spirit World

Do you believe that we are all psychic and capable of higher-level connections? If you don't, then that can be an obstacle to you reaching out to your psychic guides. Consider the following fact: we all have the ability to play the guitar if taught, but very few of us will ever be as good as Jimmy Hendrix! Fact. But we can all learn and practice to become better. The same is true regarding psychic abilities. The biggest challenge you face is overcoming the belief that you aren't psychic.

So now that the first step is out of the way, it's time to start to grow spiritually and explore the gifts your guides are waiting to send your way.

Step 1: Set Your Intentions. You will encounter this step multiple times on your journey, and that's because it is the core of successful interactions between you and your guides. They can't help you if they don't know what you want. While your spirit guardians have access to your thoughts, they are also respectful of your privacy. You must ask before you get.

Your divine plan can be as simple or as complicated as you like. Write a list of what you are expecting from your guides. Do you need protection or guidance to help you deal with negative forces? Do you lack the confidence to pursue new projects or change careers? State your dreams, desires, and wildest thoughts alongside your more practical needs and hopes. The spirits don't judge and have seen it all before; they will recognize your willingness to connect as soon as you start to ask them for help.

Step 2: Let Go of Your Practical Mind. Did you know the left side of your brain is dedicated to practical, logical, and analytic activity? When you want to become more open-minded, it will help to say goodbye to the left side of your brain. Don't forget to tell it you aren't abandoning it, and you will reconvene soon. This type of conversation is one of the first steps to changing how you think. The less open-minded you wouldn't dream of having a conversation with your brain!

Step 3: Meditate. Slowing your vibrations and opening your physical channels can be achieved with simple meditation techniques. When the spirits connect, you need to be in the best place to listen. Your first communications may be faint and difficult to understand, so you need to focus and concentrate.

Here are some simple ways to quiet your mind, nurture your inner peace, and boost your energy levels.

Focused Attention Meditation

Choose a fixed object and concentrate all your senses on it. How does it look, does it make a noise, and is there a smell associated with it? Feel the object as you close your eyes so you can feel the contours and the lines it has. Block out all other sensual interruptions and become one with your chosen object. Maintain this feeling for two minutes, and your mind will become a blank canvas for the spirits to use.

Mindful Breathing Meditation

This is a technique that needs a specified time and place to be successful. Choose a quiet place with no distractions and make yourself comfortable. Sit up straight with your spine aligned without being rigid. Take a deep breath through your nose and hold it as you relax your shoulders and arms.

Now become aware of the moment. You are in a calm place with a relaxed pose, and the moment belongs to you. Nobody else is important, and nobody else will interrupt you. Your mind is clear, and your senses are attuned to your environment.

Now breathe out through your mouth. When your breath is released, imagine it takes all negativity with it. Any guilt or regret you have ever felt, let them go. Resentment and anger will depart from you with a whoosh of breath.

Now repeat the process, and when you breathe in, imagine your body filling with love and acceptance. You are in the perfect place to receive the messages the spirits are going to send about how to fulfill your intentions and make your life better.

Loving-Kindness Meditation

This technique is also known as Metta and was taught by Buddha over 2600 years ago. Mantras are used to bring love and happiness to yourself and others. Doing this type of meditation is perfect for beginners who want to prepare for a more spiritual experience.

Choose a space that is quiet, calm, and comfortable. Sit still with your spine aligned and your arms at rest. Take a deep breath and picture the person you are sending love to.

Suggested recipients for Metta mantras

- Yourself

- Anyone who has shown you kindness or love

- Your friends

- Family members

- Random people you know who you have no personal emotions about

- Someone you have argued with or you actively dislike

15

• All living beings

Suggested mantras

• May they be filled with love and energy

• May they always be healthy and learn to heal

• Bring them peace and serenity

• May they be free from emotional and physical pain

• May they be free from suffering and heartache

As you picture the recipient of your love, chant your mantras and imagine your heart-opening. Picture the love and positivity flowing from your chest and into the person you are focusing on. Imagine the positivity growing as it transcends each being and becomes a ball of light that will eventually encompass the whole world.

Step 4: Create a Spiritual Media Room

Now your mind is primed and ready to communicate, you need to create a medium for the messages of your guides. This is your viewing receptacle and creating a movie theater in your mind is the optimum way to encourage all types of messages. Picture a huge movie screen in your mind and imagine a cord that connects it to the center of the universe. This is your grounding cord and gives you a feeling of connection to the Earth.

Now give your screen some speakers that are wired for sound. Attach them and turn up the volume ready for audio messages from the guides. Once you are seated in front of your screen, ask your questions, and wait for the answers. Never demand; just ask.

Let your answers come naturally, and then interpret them. Is the screen filled with light? Can you hear anything? Remember, the symbols and messages you will receive are from a place of truth. The spirits will never seek to misguide you because they only have the best intentions for you.

Step 5: Freewriting

This technique is often used by writers who are experiencing writers' block, and it is also great for clearing spiritual blockages. Take a pen and paper and begin writing specific statements thanking your guides for their help.

"Thank you, my spiritual team, for all you do for me and the guidance you show me in life. I recognize your spiritual compassion and love, and I invite you to join me in this journal. I welcome you to write with me and share your energies by guiding my hand and creating correspondence."

Just riff with your pen and create whatever your spirit or energy tells you. Explore subjects and experiences with words, images, or random symbols. Don't edit your work; just keep going.

Make sure you have plenty of paper as you need to make the most of your unleashed spiritual connections. Have fun with it and let your inner child loose. Make sure you go with the flow and never second guess yourself.

Connecting with the Spirits Through Your Dreams

While these are a few of the more popular ways to connect with your guides, by far, the most effective technique is through your dreams. Consider the facts. It is exceedingly rare for your mind to be fully committed to just one pursuit during the day. Family matters, work issues, and emotional ties will all be vying for your attention, so clearing your mind can be tricky.

However, when you sleep, your mind becomes more relaxed and receptive. As you enter the world of sleep, the spirits recognize you are more receptive to their messages. They will send you vivid indications within your dream and signals that will speak to you. Different images and sensations will mean different things to individuals, but some recurring images have common spiritual interpretations.

The basic meanings listed below will help you understand what the spirits are telling you, and then you can apply them to your particular circumstances and needs:

- **Flying:** By far the most common types of dreams. When you dream of soaring in the skies without being on board an airplane, it indicates positivity. The guides are congratulating you for your creativity and spiritual maturity. Dreams like this are a spiritual pat on the back and indicate you are on the right path.

- **Beaches:** Do you ever dream you are on a sandy beach with the waves lapping at your toes? This is a positive sign you are connected to your spiritual team as it is a representation of the place between heaven and Earth. Beaches that seem too idyllic to be real are a sign they hear you and are sending other signs to help you navigate your life.

- **School or tests:** When you dream about taking a test or attending classes, the spirits are telling you now is the time to expand your knowledge. This means you should take on classes to help you progress at work and in your personal life. This type of dream means you are ready to make a move to a higher level of spiritual maturity. Make a note of what grade you are in during your dream, as this will give you an indication of where you are currently.

- **Teeth falling out or coming loose:** In natural life, our teeth chew our food and make it easier to digest. In spiritual terms, problems with teeth indicate problems with digesting information. The spirits are telling you to seek direction or advice in your physical world.

• **Being pregnant or giving birth:** Both men and women can have these dreams. They are the symbol of rebirth and moving on from the past. This could be a new job, a budding relationship, or a sign of inventiveness. Giving birth is one of the most symbolic messages you will receive.

• **Car journeys:** The first thing to note is where you are sitting on the journey. Are you the driver, or are you the passenger? Driving is a symbol of leadership and authority and signals you are firmly in charge. You have your destination clearly defined, and the journey is well underway. Passengers are more indicative that you are happy to be led by others. If you feel uncomfortable in the passenger seat, it is an indication you need to become more assertive and take the lead.

• **Falling:** When you dream of falling without support, it is a signal to get a grip. You are spiraling out of control and need some peace in your life. This type of dream will often repeat itself night after night until you regain the peace you need.

- **Paralysis:** When you dream that you are stuck in a place and unable to move on, it is a sign that dark forces are affecting you. If you can't call out or speak and the world is passing you by, it's a sign you are stuck in a rut. You need to move on and fulfill your wildest dreams. Resistance isn't always a bad thing; it is just another obstacle to make you work harder.

- **Weather:** Different weather patterns are a clear sign from the spirits. Dreaming of rain and stormy outbursts means you are about to receive a barrage of messages from your guides. They feel you are ready for them and open to their communications. Good weather like sunshine, bright skies, and gentle breezes mean they are already with you.

- **Being naked in public:** Dreaming about your nakedness in public is relatively common. When these dreams occur, the spirits are telling you that your shortcomings are threatening to take over your life. You aren't real with your relationships, and it's time to examine your authentic self and release a more genuine side of your personality.

- **Being chased:** When you are being pursued, it's important to note who is doing the chasing. If the figure is unidentified, it signals the presence of past trauma and a childhood experience. The spirits are telling you to get help to overcome these influences and move on. If the figure chasing you is the opposite sex, it signals you are being held back by a previous relationship or your reluctance to let others into your life. Being chased by an animal indicates you are overly wary of your emotions. It's time to embrace your passions as well as your fears.

• **Dreams about death:** These types of dreams can be incredibly disconcerting because we rarely think of our own mortality and death. If you are dreaming of the death of a loved one who has passed, then it is a direct communication from their spirit to tell you they are happy and at peace in the spirit world. If the death is less specific, it means you are afraid of change.

Some studies have shown that vivid dreams with significant details and meanings will happen when people are reaching the end of their lives. The spirits will use dreams to comfort and prepare them for their journey. Dreams can be a sign of change and should be studied with as much detail as possible.

A dream journal will help you analyze these signs and messages from the spirit world. When you wake, note the details of your dreams with as much detail as possible.

• Who was in your dreams, and what were they doing?

• What time of year was it, and what was the weather like?

• How did your dream make you feel?

• How old were you in the dream?

• Was there any sound to accompany your visual experience?

• Did you feel like it was really happening, or did you know it was a dream?

The more details you have, the more relevant your messages will become. Don't forget that you will improve with practice, and your dreams will become clearer as you get better at interpreting them. You may like to consult with a dream expert and learn the meanings they assign to your nocturnal messages for a broader spectrum of knowledge.

Chapter 3: How to Stay Safe During Spiritual Communications

Popular media and other forms of entertainment have been caught up in the paranormal and reaching the other side for decades. However, the concept of communicating with the astral plane goes back further than the invention of movies and television. People have been attempting to contact "the other side" for centuries and, as such, have developed some effective ways of protecting themselves against negative energies.

When you consider protecting yourself before reaching out, it's important to understand what you are protecting yourself against. Are there malignant spirits out there? Of course, there are. After all, the spirit world doesn't judge who enters its realms. Even spirits with lower energy and less developed spiritual awakening play a role. They are needed to become guides to those who need them because they are following the same path the spirits did in life.

People who aren't ready to cast off their more salubrious lifestyles still need spiritual guidance, and spirits with less energy will fulfill those roles. However, as a more enlightened soul, you don't want them bringing their negative vibes to your world, so you need protection.

The Best Techniques to Protect Yourself from Negative Energies

You must prepare yourself before you begin to attract your spirit guides. The experience can be overwhelming if you aren't fully prepared. Grounding, centering, and shielding are three of the more successful ways to make sure you only receive love and strength from your spirit group.

Centering

Different spiritual beliefs and traditions have different definitions regarding centering, so you must find the best technique for yourself. The basics are much the same in all teachings, so use them to create your own ritual that covers the areas you need.

Step 1) Create a quiet space. At home, turn off all your electrical devices and lock the doors. If you're outdoors, make sure the only interruptions are from the breeze and the swing of the trees.

Step 2) Choose a comfortable seating position. You can lie down, but some people find they drift off to sleep when supine.

Step 3) Take a deep breath and relax. Concentrate on your breathing and use a chant to regulate your breath.

Step 4) Visualize energy. Once your breathing is regulated, it's time to create an energy field. Rub your palms together as if you were trying to warm your hands and then pull them slightly apart. You will feel a tingling sensation that crackles between your palms.

Step 5) Now it's time to expand your thoughts. Imagine that energy field traveling around your whole body. Feel it expand and contract as it swirls around you. Now imagine it is a ball of energy that can travel between your hands and throw it from one hand to the other.

Once you have mastered this technique, you will be able to use it wherever you are. Stuck on a bus or trapped in a boring meeting? Use this to center yourself and re-energize your core.

Grounding

When you contact spirits, you are encountering energy levels you rarely encounter on an earthly plane. Keeping yourself prepared for these encounters is simple, yet essential. Grounding is a process where you learn how to rid your body of excess energy safely and in a controlled manner. Centering is all about creating energy, while grounding is all about dispelling it.

You need to master how to get rid of unwanted energy without projecting it into others. Following a spiritual ritual or connection, you will often feel jittery and out of kilter with the physical world. This is because you have amped your energies up, and they are interfering with your senses.

Grounding is fairly simple and requires just a few practice sessions. Close your eyes and focus on the energy gathered in your solar plexus. Imagine it as a ball of fire and light, and push it into your hands. Now imagine you are shaking your hands, and the energy is leaving your body and shooting into the ground. You should choose an object or container to contain your energy and keep it safe. Try a bucket of angry sand to stand outside your door when you feel the need to shed your excess energy, project it into your bucket and keep it away from your home.

Another method is to push the energy down through your legs and into your feet. Imagine a removable plug at the soles of your feet that can be pulled to let the energy go. It will drain into the ground, where it is absorbed by nature. Some people find it helpful to jump up and down to get rid of that last piece of residual energy.

Both techniques of grounding will benefit from an oral cheer. Shouting something such as "Begone you pesky energies" will help finish the exercise with vigor. Of course, you can create your own cheer to release these pent-up energies.

Spiritual Shielding

Shielding is a popular term used to cover forms of protection in the metaphysical world, and it includes many different methods. You should employ as many of these shielding techniques as you like. Your protection is paramount, and the need to keep negative energy away is essential.

• Create an energy field

When you expel energy during a grounding session, you can use it differently. Rather than casting it off, use the excess forces to create a powerful shield to protect you from malignant spirits. As the energy leaves your fingertips, imagine it flowing over your physical body and forming a bubble of protection. When you look at the exterior of your bubble, you will notice that it's reflective and impervious. This shield will be your ultimate safe place where only high-level spirits will be allowed.

• Crystals

Protective crystals are a great way to employ a portable protection system. Black crystals are impressive when used to form a shield, but many others have amazing properties of protection. Emeralds, lapis lazuli, clear quartz, and tiger eye crystals are all readily available and are all potent forms of deflecting unwanted energies.

• Invoking the spirits of protection

Jesus and his archangels are there for you. This has nothing to do with your religion or beliefs. We will talk about the archangels in a later chapter, but Jesus will always send you the light of protection when you need it. Remember, you only have to ask.

• Mirrored jewelry

Just like you see the protective qualities of your reflective surface that covers your energy field, you can use mirrors to deflect negativity. Place small hand mirrors around yourself to provide a refractive surface. Wear a mirrored pendant around your neck for extra layers of strength.

• Cut the cord

Despite the layers of protection, you surround yourself with, there is a remote possibility your personal space will be penetrated. You need to know how to get rid of any energies you don't feel comfortable with. This doesn't just apply to your spiritual connections; sometimes, negative physical relationships will interfere with your attempts to grow spiritually.

How to perform a cord-cutting ritual to remove negativity from physical relationships:

Decide who needs to be removed from your auric field. These can be people from your past who are still interfering with your thoughts and causing you distress. They are also people who are in your present environment and need to be removed. Make a list of anybody who qualifies as a negative force. Include past partners who have caused you distress or cheated on you. Include anyone who abused or bullied you in your formative years or people in your workplace who don't treat you with respect.

Now, invoke the spirits and your spiritual guide to help you remove the etheric cords that bind you to these people. Name them and state your intent to separate your energies from theirs. State the following with power and intent or form your own version to appeal to the spirits:

"I compel my loving spirit family and all accompanying angels and guides to come forward and help me cut the etheric cords that bind me to (insert name/names.) I forgive and bless them with the ability to live in peace, and I release them to move away as I shall also do."

"I ask you to break all energy cords and transmute the debris into a cosmic place or return it to the person who first created it. I bear no ill will to (inset name/names), and I wish them spiritual peace and conscious uncoupling."

Once the ritual is over, you should spend a few minutes feeling the powers begin to work. Some people will find a shift in their energy levels immediately, while others will take longer. If you perform the ritual just before you go to sleep, you may experience significant and vivid dreams about the people you have cut the cord from. These will be the last time these energies will be part of your life so remember to thank your angels and spirits for their intervention the following morning.

How to cleanse your space and make it sacred:

We all need to know that there is a place where we feel ultimately safe and protected. This may be a room, a place in the garden, or a simple piece of furniture. This haven is where you can go to talk to your spirits and ask them questions. You know that when your sacred space is in use, you are sending out a signal to the universe that you are engaged and ready to communicate.

Your sacred space should be an oasis in a chaotic world. Make sure you bring supplies like a blanket in case you feel cold, and drinks in case you feel thirsty. You never know how long you will be there as our timeline doesn't govern the spirits, and they may have a lot to say!

Create a space that contains elements of Earth. This means representing the basic elements of Air, Fire, Water, and Earth. Be imaginative and decorate your space with items that are aesthetically pleasing and bring you joy.

Air is generally represented by feathers, wind chimes, or a fan. Place your items in the East and use the upside-down triangle with a horizontal line through it to further strengthen the connection.

Candles and other forms of light represent fire. You could also use solar lights for safety or incense to create a connection with this particular element. An upright triangle is a representative symbol of fire. Place your symbols in the Southern part of your space.

Water is the element you can have real fun with. Seashells, seawater, or a bowl of sacred, blessed water will represent the aspect water brings to life. Place your items in the Western part of your space.

Earth is the element that supports us and creates a rock for us. Represent this by using plants or stones to decorate and protect your space. Put your items in the Northern part of your space.

Do a spiritual clean by smudging your space. Dried herbs, sage, and rosemary are perfect for burning and casting cleansing smoke into your space.

The key to creating your sacred space is to avoid overcomplicating things. Keep it simple and tailored to your needs. Your sacred space is yours. Don't let others pollute it with their energies and negativity.

Chapter 4: Why Do We Need Spirit Guides?

Consider your life; from birth through childhood and into adulthood, nobody has a clear path without obstacles. Everybody must make decisions and deal with traumatic experiences. Sure, the people that surround us will be there for us, but a higher force is needed to help and support us. Some people believe they have been reincarnated several times, and this helps them grow spiritually, while others believe that we are only here once, and you should make the most of your time on Earth.

No matter what your beliefs are, you are going to get a helping hand from the spiritual world whether you want it or not. This help will only become more powerful when you fuel it with your intentions and strive to contact those who form your spiritual group. Knowing when to do so can be controversial, and some people will attempt to make contact for all the wrong reasons.

There are several reasons you may feel compelled to contact the spiritual world. You can do so through a medium or by initiating contact through yourself. Whatever method you choose, if you are doing it for the right reason, then the outcome will be rewarding and successful.

The Right Reasons to Connect with the Spirit World

• You have lost a loved one and feel you need to connect with them. Perhaps you have unfinished business you need to resolve, or they expressed a desire to connect with you after death. While this is probably the most common reason for reaching out to the spirits, that doesn't mean it is always a good idea. Don't try and settle scores with people who have passed on. Only initiate connections if you are committed to positive experiences. The spirit world is not the place to bring grudges and arguments that can't be resolved.

• You have always felt you have connections with the spiritual realm. People who are born with mediumship tendencies will know from an early age that they have a gift. Their dreams will be filled with clear messages from the astral realm, and they will have encounters with spirits during their waking hours as well. Catching a glimpse of someone who has passed away is a clear sign that you have the skill to bridge the gap between the living world and the realm of the spirits.

• If you have seen things that are out of the ordinary, it may be a sign the spirit world seeks to connect with you. Feathers appearing from nowhere or butterflies in the depth of winter are just a couple of examples of spiritual communications. In your heart, you will know when the time is right; after all, the spirits have some control over what your gut tells you is right.

• Modern society and the world you live in are becoming hectic and overwhelming. Seeking a more peaceful life is a valid reason for connecting with your spiritual group. You should create a sacred space to retreat to where you can forget the fast-paced environment you live in and visit a place that is filled with harmony, peace, and love. Some people retreat to nature when it all gets too much to handle; you will retreat to the ultimate nature within the astral realm.

The Wrong Reasons to Seek Connection with the Spirit World

Whenever there are good reasons to do something, there must also be bad reasons. Connecting to the spirits is no different. Popular media have been obsessed with mediums, exorcists, evil spirits, and the rest for decades. They fill the publics' heads with misinformation, and their images can fuel people to delve into the supernatural for the wrong reasons.

Communicating with the other side is an option that's available to everyone, but certain boundaries shouldn't be crossed. This is a serious subject and should not be undertaken lightly or on a whim. Every connection is a sacred and powerful bond that should be respected. The spirits are not there to be a plaything for humans; they are there for a higher purpose.

- You are unprepared. Nobody wakes up one morning and spontaneously decides they are spiritual and want to connect with a higher force. There is a build-up before any example of the true intent, and this takes time. You should never begin communications without the right preparation and a strong form of protection.

- It is being used as part of the entertainment at a social gathering. How many stories of Ouija boards being used at slumber parties have you heard? Did it ever go well? No, and it never will. Holding a séance at a social party is not a great idea either. Spiritual communication is all based on energies, so imagine what a maelstrom of energies can be found at a social gathering where people drink, socialize with strangers, or seek to be frightened by evil spirits. You have no control over other people's intentions or emotions, so you could be putting yourself at risk.

- You have been dared to join in. When someone is pushing your buttons, it can be easy to make bad decisions which are okay sometimes but not in this situation. Don't let your ego get the better of you; walk away if you don't feel comfortable, and never feel pressured to join in. Leave the others or stay and talk them out of it; the choice is yours. Whatever your decision, you are only responsible for your personal safety, and that should be your priority.

• It looks cool on television and in the movies. If this is your primary reason for contacting the spirit world, it probably won't work. Go back to watching films and shows about spirits and leave it at that. If you have been truly inspired by something on the screen, then you will do your research and take the subject seriously.

Now we have established the reasoning for your choice to connect or not; it's time to look at some simple dos and don'ts. If you are in the right frame of mind and prepared mentally and physically for the connection, then follow this list of what to do before you begin:

• Protect yourself. A basic form of protection is to invite your spiritual team to join you. You may not have met them yet, but they are there.

• Dress appropriately. Keep your clothing light and cool so it doesn't distract you. You need to be focused on your mental state, and fiddling with straps or sleeves will only deviate your thoughts and lessen your intention. A pair of comfortable leisurewear bottoms topped with a cotton tee shirt is perfect.

• Prepare for the encounter beforehand. Write a letter to your spirit guide. State what you hope to achieve and how much you are looking forward to meeting them. Using this method of communication means you can be more precise about what you expect from the encounter.

• Ask what the spirit is called. When you communicate with them, it's a two-way conversation. People often make the mistake of believing the spirits are there to tell them what to do, how to do it, and why. You should expect a full and frank discussion just like you would in your physical relationships. Just because they are spirits doesn't mean they are superior to you. Treat them as your contemporaries and bounce your ideas off them.

• Use the correct tools to strengthen your connections. Tools like tarot cards, pendulums, and automatic writing implements don't work for everyone, but you will never know if you don't try. Tools help you focus your intentions.

Now for the don'ts! You must note these points because there are low-level spirits you don't want to encounter, so your intentions need to be correct and pure:

• Don't use tools that appeal to you just because you've seen them on the television or in film. Ouija or spirit boards are not ideal for beginners as they can be dangerous to use. Using more traditional healthy tools will keep you safe, while a Ouija board could allow negativity and bad energies to infect your space.

• Don't expect whistles and bells from your encounter. You may be lucky and see your spirit guide in a physical form, or you may just get an essence of your spirit. This can be a subtle smell or feeling that indicates they are with you. As with all things worth doing, you will get better with practice. Don't be disillusioned or disheartened if your spirit isn't as accessible as you would like. Remember, they need to use their energies to communicate, and you must be patient with the process.

• Don't carry on with a spiritual encounter if something feels off. Listen to your intuition and be prepared to walk away. There is no limit to the number of times you can reach out to the astral plane, so there is no harm in retreating if you feel overwhelmed.

• Don't force issues. This is a fluid form of communication, and you should be prepared to go with the flow. You may have certain intentions, yet the messages you receive are dedicated to other areas of your life. Don't think the guides are deliberately ignoring your initial concerns; they probably recognize that other areas of your life require more immediate attention before you can move on.

• Don't come with preconceived ideas. If you begin your spiritual journey with a predetermined idea of what is going to happen and how your life is going to improve overnight, you may be disappointed. The spirits have your back, but they are not the route to material wealth or success unless you deserve it. Asking a spirit to tell you next week's lottery numbers only show disrespect and mockery for their world.

• Don't be confrontational with your spirit guides. It may look cool on the television and be entertaining to watch, but in reality, it's just asking for trouble. Yes, you can ask questions, but ridiculing or teasing a spirit will never end well. Again, you need to treat your team with love and respect.

Now you have a fuller understanding of what you can expect from spiritual encounters; you are in the perfect frame of mind to decide what to do next. Should you start to commune with the spirits yourself, or should you consult the professionals first?

If you choose to use a medium, make sure they are reputable and have checkable referrals. Do you want messages about your future and what direction you need to choose? Then you should choose a psychic rather than a medium.

Price should also be considered. Most mediums are more interested in their subjects than the financial aspects, but they do need to make a living. Choose a medium that is stating a fair hourly rate based on their experience. $50-60 per hour is about right for experienced mediums with a good track record.

Chapter 5: Spiritual Signs and How to Interpret Them

Have you ever noticed random items appearing in your life that make you feel good? You can't pinpoint why you feel better; you just do. Chances are your spiritual guides are communicating with you because they feel you need them.

Here are some of the most common ways the spirits communicate with us and what they are saying:

Feathers

Have you ever wondered why native people wear brightly colored feathers as part of their traditional garb? Why do they paint images of feathers on their walls and incorporate them into their native rituals? Many cultures believe that feathers are a significant way for spirits to communicate with us and that they appear to carry an important message from the universe.

Finding a feather is a magical moment, and they represent freedom and the ability to soar above the physical world. When you receive a feather as a sign, it can mean many different things. Did you subconsciously ask for help, or did the feather just appear out of the blue? How do you know if it's a sign or just something a bird has shed?

Chances are the feather will appear in an unusual place and will appear directly in front of you. These types of signs often appear at the doorway of your home or on a piece of clothing. You will know when a magical sign is sent because of the feelings it evokes.

What Do the Feather Colors Mean?

White

Somebody is watching over you. Your guardian angel will often send you a white feather to let you know they have your back. White signifies a form of protection from above and will bring you joy and love. White feathers are also connected to lunar energy that will instill a sense of purity and peace.

Red

This is the color of the root chakra and signifies passion and energy. The spirits are gifting you the courage and vitality to get you through troubling times. Red feathers appear to show you that good fortune is in your future. Red is also the color of love, so your spirits are telling you that your relationship will be okay, providing you bring energy and passion.

Blue

This color is representative of the throat chakra. The spirits are telling you to speak your truth and be heard. They are sending you a sign that you should be more self-appreciative and less negative about yourself.

Yellow

This is the representative color of the solar plexus chakra. Yellow feathers are a sign of wisdom and a connection to solar energies, and the spirits are blessing you with wisdom and joy while they remind you that you can be a bit too serious. Embrace your playful side and be more cheerful. You can sometimes get wrapped up in profound matters and forget to let go and enjoy life.

Green

This is the color of the heart chakra. As such, it represents love, emotions, and relationships. It signifies a period of fertility and birth. Green also signals that nature's healing benefits are looking out for you, and you should connect with living organisms and flora.

Orange

This is the color of the sacral chakra, and it represents creation and energy. The spirits are indicating your sexual energies, and your attractions will be heightened soon. You are about to encounter strong physical love and energy. Make sure you embrace any chance of connecting with a positive complementary force of nature.

Pink

This colored feather is sent to remind you that the spirits are always there for you. They have unconditional love and friendship that you can rely on, no matter what happens. The universe is sending you a sign that you are blessed with its love and support.

Gray

This is the color of faith. Spirits are telling you to believe in yourself and know that even the most troublesome problem will be solved in time. A pair of gray feathers means that they recognize the traumas you are currently undergoing, and they are working on the solution. Hang on in there and be assured that better times lie ahead.

Purple

This is the color of the crown chakra, which forms your central consciousness. A purple feather is sent to remind you just how connected you are to your spiritual self. It also means you are ready to improve your connections and ascend to a higher plane.

Brown

The color of the Earth. A brown feather is a sign that you should ground yourself and improve your sense of home. You may be unconsciously neglecting your family and forgetting to nurture your friendships. A brown feather is a gentle reminder to respect your roots and give them the attention they deserve.

Black

The color black is often misunderstood when it comes to spiritual meanings. While it can be a serious warning from the spirits, it is also a sign of protection from the universe. A shiny black feather represents the spirits giving you a high five regarding your spiritual development. It is sent to congratulate you on your progress and remind you that your quest for spiritual insight is well on track.

The next time you are sent a feather, remember to give thanks. Stop what you are doing and say a prayer or a heartfelt thanks to the universe for its message. Keep your feathers in a sacred place like an altar or arrange them so they are visible. They are meant to be admired and will act as a reminder that your spirits are always with you.

Other Significant Signs the Spirits are Communicating with You

1) A breeze suddenly appears.

Have you ever felt a splash of fresh air on an otherwise still day? A gentle caress of air means the spirits are blessing you with a tranquil reminder they are there for you. When you feel this sensation, look around and check if anything else is affected by the breeze. Are the leaves moving, or is it just you? This type of contact is one of the most comforting signs; embrace it and be uplifted.

2) Music suddenly appears that has special significance for you.

We all have special songs that remind us of certain times and emotions. When the universe is trying to bring us comfort, it will send us a song to remind us of better times. Songs that relate to your situation are a common way for spirits to send us messages.

3) Visitors from nature

The spirits are especially good at using natural forces for messaging us on Earth. Butterflies, swallows, eagles, foxes, and owls are all imbued with meaning, as are myriad other animals. When you encounter a natural force in an unusual place, you are being sent a message to comfort you and bring you joy.

4) You reconnect with someone from your past

The spirits love to use past connections to deliver their messages. If you bump into someone or get a call from a person you haven't seen for years, make sure you take notice of the conversation. They will undoubtedly have some pertinent things to tell you. Take notice and act on the information you receive.

5) You get the sensation that someone is watching you

This is a common feeling amongst those who are actively manifesting their desires. Spirits love to give you a physical sense of their presence by creating a sensation of protection. When you form a connection with the universe, it loves to remind you it's keeping an eye out for you.

6) Advice from random sources

Have you ever turned the television or radio on and been amazed by the subject of the program? You just happen to tune into a financial advice program when you are experiencing monetary woes or randomly come across an advertisement for financial help. Billboards, media sources, and other random sources can contain messages from the spirits. Some call it a coincidence, while others realize its providence from above.

7) Unexpected gifts from serendipitous sources

Have good things been happening to you lately? Are you experiencing a succession of days when everything goes your way? Guess what? The spirits are telling you that you deserve the absolute best. Feeling lucky and blessed is a great gift from the spirits. Remember to thank them for their interventions and recognize the gifts they have bestowed on you.

8) Synchronicity of numbers

Everyday life is filled with numerical encounters. You pay bills, shop at the store, check the time and date, and every encounter provides the spirits with a chance to communicate. Numerology is a powerful way to interpret what those messages are telling you, so understanding the significance of numbers is vital.

The Spiritual Meaning of Numbers

1) The number one represents independence and creativity. This number says that you are more of a leader than a follower, and that you are a free spirit. When the number is repeated, it signifies the opening of a spiritual gateway for you to connect with the universe and develop to your maximum potential with its help.

2) The number two represents the presence of masculine and feminine energy. It signals harmony and balance, and when repeated, it means your life is at a harmonious place. The spirits are telling you that your desires and manifestations are close to fruition.

3) The number three is a representation of the mind, body, and soul. The spirits are assuring you that you are ready to grow and expand. When the number is repeated, it signals the absence of conflict and gives you the green light to work on your spirituality.

4) The number four is associated with inner strength and prosperity. Multiple fours mean that you will be

successful in business matters and in creating something beneficial to others.

5) The number five is a symbol of freedom and happiness. Multiple fives signal that change is coming and the spirits are telling you to prepare for a wave of positivity entering your life.

6) The number six is an indication that you should be humbler. The spirits love your self-confidence, but they are telling you to reign it in and be a bit more grounded. Repeated sixes mean they are encouraging you to listen to your inner voice and use your intellect.

7) The number seven is related to spiritual health and enlightenment. The spirits will use repeated examples of sevens to remind you to work on your spiritual development and awareness. Triple seven is a powerful sign that good fortune, luck, and even miracles are heading your way.

8) The number eight represents the solid, dependable part of you. Repeated eights are signals that your universal energy will be best used to improve practical matters, like your finances. Triple eight represents a natural flow of wealth and prosperity.

9) The number nine signifies completion. When you see this number or multiples of nine, it is a sign that something must give. You must let go of one area of your life so that others can grow. Double nine is a signal from the universe to think about how you can be of service to others. Any multiples of nines are indicative of the closing of a chapter and the need for compassion.

Chapter 6: Archangels

Who are Archangels?

Not to be confused with guardian angels, these heavenly bodies are a direct link to the celestial powers. If you are a Christian, this is the entity you know as God, and if you belong to different religious groups, they are connected to the highest spirit or deity within your belief system.

Despite their elevated status, it isn't difficult to invoke them. They are there to help and will welcome your communications. You can ask them to intervene in your life by praying to them and mentally asking for their assistance. You can converse with them verbally, or you can write them a letter to state your intentions. Be prepared for a major force to enter your life when you invoke Archangels.

Like other spiritual guides, each of the Archangels has a specific purpose and area they specialize in. This doesn't mean you can't contact them about more generic subjects, but understanding their strengths will give you a better chance at finding the answers you need. They can help you with their wisdom, and they will fight in your corner whenever you need them.

In the Bible, Archangels are credited with immense powers and are responsible for governing lesser angels. If you need a powerhouse of the spiritual realm, then call on these influential members of the astral world.

What Do the Different Archangels Represent?

The first thing to understand is that most representations of Archangels depict them as a certain gender. In truth, they will adopt the gender that fits the situation.

Archangel Gabriel

The name Gabriel means God is my strength which gives you an indication of the power this Archangel wields. He is the supreme messenger and will help you if you are finding it difficult to communicate clearly with your spiritual team. Call on him for a clearer way to interpret messages from above and be blessed by his power and love.

Archangel Michael

This warrior angel is often depicted bearing a sword and shield. He is the ultimate protector and will fight for you when you're under psychic attacks. If you have dragons that need slaying, you want Michael in your corner. He is the most powerful angel in the celestial realm, and on the day of judgment, it will be his responsibility to weigh all human souls on the scales of justice.

Archangel Raphael

His name means one who heals, so turn to Raphael if you are dealing with sickness or ill health. He deals with all types of sickness and suffering in the physical, emotional, and mental forms. He is filled with compassion and comfort and will come to your aid if you need comfort and care.

Archangel Ariel

The Lioness of God. Let this powerful force into your life when you are affected by environmental issues. Ariel is a champion of nature and will help you deal with your concerns about ecological matters and injured animals. She is the ultimate eco-warrior, and her power will bring you the strength to campaign for a better world.

Archangel Haniel

Her name means the joy of God. Call upon her when you need help to connect to your higher self. She is responsible for protecting your soul, so invoke her powers if you feel internally bruised and need to heal. She will help you heal and overcome destructive and damaging emotional swings.

Archangel Metatron

The angel of life Metatron is responsible for the tree of life. His duties include recording the good deeds people do and helping children to grow into adulthood. If you want to explore your potential psychic and spiritual gifts, contact Metatron, and ask for his help to develop your skills. If you have a big decision to make, call upon Metatron to give you advice.

Archangel Jophiel

She is known as the beauty of God and is especially associated with creativity and artistic talents. She has a powerful vibration and will bring calm to those who are in turmoil. Use her to bring joy to your life whenever you are feeling negative or sad.

Archangel Muriel

Her name means the perfume of God. She brings compassion and love to those who need it. Muriel will help anyone who needs her, and once you establish the connection, you will feel like you have made a new friend. Call on her when you need emotional support.

Archangel Uriel

The angel of wisdom. He will be your guiding light in dark times. His wisdom and insight will help you develop your perceptions and solve your problems. He is one of the illuminated seraphim, which means he has a direct link to the Creator and can help you form bonds with the spiritual world.

Archangel Azrael

The angel of death. Use him as your spiritual counselor in times of grief and loss; if your anger and negativity have reached the point where your feel capable of harming someone, then reach out to Azrael for his guidance. He will help you get back to a good place in life and let go of the negative emotions you are harboring.

Archangel Zadkiel

The angel of forgiveness and mercy. He is a powerful force who can help you let go of the past and become spiritually reborn. He will bring you the strength to cleanse your soul and raise your vibrations by forgiving you and setting you free to become the person you want to be. If you are stuck in a rut and want to move forward, Zadkiel will come to your aid.

Archangel Chamuel

The angel of peaceful relationships. Call on him to bring calm to any relationship situations that have got out of hand. The physical relationships you have are important, but he will also help you deal with spiritual bonds.

Archangel Jeremiel

This is a unique Archangel. He is one of the original seven responsible for overseeing humanity and serving their needs. He is not a vocal angel but prefers to communicate through dreams and other non-verbal methods. He loves to guide and teach us, but he will send his messages through symbols, dreams, and visions. His influence over your subconscious mind means he is always with you when you need him.

Archangel Raziel

He is the angel of secret and is one of God's right-hand men. He guards the mystery of the universe and is privy to the most innate knowledge regarding it. His knowledge isn't gained easily; he believes that if you want to become more spiritually grounded, then you must work for it. His calm and collected nature means he will often remain undetected, but be sure that he wants you to succeed and will do everything in his power to help you.

Archangel Sandalphon

He is the guardian of nature and is a direct link to earthly forces. He revels in music and joy, making him one of the easiest Archangels to work with. He has a down-to-earth persona that makes him approachable and provides a direct path to the heavens. Because of his approachability, Sandalphon is the perfect Archangel for beginners. He will welcome you with open arms and help you feel comfortable in the higher realms.

Archangel Sachiel

He is a relatively unknown name in modern records of Archangels. His name is associated with the planet Jupiter which is the largest planet in the solar system. This is because he is the angel of growth and success. He can help you in matters of personal success, prosperity, and material gain. These may not seem like angelic areas, but at times, we all need help to be successful. Call on him to help you expand your thoughts, take

Archangel Orion

Associated with the star Orion, he is considered the least ostentatious of all the Archangels. He is new at interacting with humans and prefers to keep his messages non-verbal. His main aim is to help you drop your inhibitions and be inspired to grow and expand. He brings a unique vibration to your life and can be relied on to help your dreams come true.

Connecting with Archangels may sound like a major spiritual step. It will take immense courage to reach out to these important spiritual beings for some people, yet it will come easily for others. Remember, your religious affiliations don't matter when it comes to the Archangels; they will help you no matter what your beliefs are.

They have the powers to access your thoughts and can be trusted to keep them private. You don't need to perform special rituals to invoke their help; you just need an open mind. Once you feel the telepathic powers the angels will send you, it is a signal that they recognize your needs and are on the job.

You will soon recognize that some Archangels work better in tandem with others. For instance, Orion and Sachiel both concentrate their powers on success and material wealth. Bring them into your spiritual team and feel the difference almost immediately. You will have the self-confidence and inner strength to achieve your dreams and become a more successful human because of their help.

The Book of Life tells us that Sandalphon and Metatron are brothers, so their power is intertwined. Study the characteristics and powers of all the Archangels, and you will benefit from their interventions even more. Don't expect the process to bring you visions and messages immediately, as your technique will improve with practice. As with all spiritual communications, the first step is to give your permission for contact. Once you have opened your mind to them, they will respond.

Chapter 7: Spirit Animals

The spirits that guard us will take many forms when they visit us. They intuitively know how to make us feel calm and protected by taking a natural form, usually an animal or bird. These spirit forms are often bundled together as "spirit animals,' but there are different meanings behind certain spirits.

You must decide what these symbols of nature mean and determine the message they bring. This will make sense when applied to the present, past, or future events and the emotions they trigger. You must understand that you can't choose your spirit animal or when it will make an appearance in your life. These are already preordained and will happen when the time is right.

You may feel like you are more associated with the mighty lion or a powerful bear, yet you keep seeing butterflies and ducks rather than the mighty beasts you think you are connected to. Just believe in the process and let it flow naturally. The spirits will assign you the right animal at the right time. These will change as your situation and maturity evolve. Specific phases of your life will be represented by the animals that are relevant to your needs.

You may feel an affinity to certain animals depending on your birthday. If you were born under Aries or Capricorn, you would feel an affinity to Caprine animals like the ram and the goat. Sheep and other breeds with cloven hooves will intrigue you. Piscine animals will appeal to those born under water signs, while the lions and other big cats appeal to people born under the sign of Leo.

But what if your zodiac sign doesn't have connections to the animal world like Gemini or Virgo? These signs are more likely to find a connection with mythical fantasy animals like the phoenix or Bigfoot. There are no hard and fast rules concerning spirit animals, and you will get your connection based on your personality, your spiritual needs, and what traits the animal can bring to your world.

There is no spiritual snobbery involved here. The smallest insect is just as powerful as the mighty giraffe. Remember, we are all part of the great tapestry we call life, and we all have an important role to play. If you are drawn to fireflies, then go with it!

Spirit, Totem, and Power Animals

Spirit Animals

Do you see repeated examples of particular animals wherever you look? Do you randomly see documentaries about them and then see a piece of art featuring their image? Are they part of an advertisement that seems to appear on the television between every program you watch? This is likely your spirit animal.

Effectively, these spirit forms are a representation of the powers and skills you currently have. They are sent to remind you of your power to grow, expand, and better yourself by learning. They also represent messages regarding different people or situations you are currently involved with.

For instance, a slow-moving animal like a tortoise or sloth will be sent to tell you to slow down and reconsider any serious decisions you have made recently. A spirit bird will visit you if the spirits believe it's time for you to spread your wings. How you interpret your spirit animals is up to you, but having a general knowledge of what they represent will help.

Totem Animals

Do you have a collection of items that relates to a particular animal? You know you have too many, but you simply must feel compelled to buy everything you can get your hands on? This is your totem animal that speaks to your soul. In Native American culture, the tradition dictated that your totem animal stays with you and your family for life. When you grow spiritually, your knowledge of your totem animal will also grow.

Power Animals

If you have never heard the term Biomimicry or Biomimetics, then you may not have experienced the connection with power animals. In native cultures, the elders teach children from an early age to call upon the animal kingdom to help them learn how to develop. Potential hunters would call upon the tiger or panther to "become" like them when they hunt.

The spirit of the animal would guide the children to master the activity and give them the knowledge they need. For instance, a squirrel would be called upon to bring a sense of fun, while a hawk would help to get a better view of a situation.

Calling in your power animal is a natural process. DNA connects all humans and animals, and all of us have the power to harness the knowledge we seek. Call forth or invoke the spirit of your required power animal to bestow their energy and strength whenever you feel the need.

The animals you communicate with come from a diverse ecological system, so they could be insects, mammals, fish, amphibians, or birds. Alternatively, the spirit world may decide to send you representations from the world of fantasy and mythological creatures. Every form of life represents something, so expect to see more diverse creatures as your spiritual self grows and becomes finely attuned to the messages you receive.

Here are some examples of creatures and animals who will appear as spirit animals and who can be called forth as power animals:

Amphibians and Reptiles

These hardy creatures are closely affiliated with water and exist in a world that is split between land and water. As such, they represent the two elements of Earth and water. They will appear to you when you feel disconnected from your true feelings. They are a symbol to tell you it's time to let go and release some pent-up feelings.

If you have a reptile or amphibian totem animal in your life, it means you have love and warmth. You are fiercely independent and will often have psychic abilities.

As a power animal, call on reptiles and amphibians for personal development and help to develop your spiritual senses. They will assist you when you need to ramp up your energy levels and amplify your spiritual voice.

One of the most popular and common amphibian spirits is the frog. If you see images and representations of frogs, it can signal many things. It often means you are influenced by physical appearance and are missing out on love because of this. Frogs tell us to take time to know people and discover their inner beauty.

A frog's appearance is also an indication of prosperity and abundant times for you and your family. Your frog spirit is telling you to take care of yourself and detoxify your life. It is also a symbol of fertility and rebirth.

Other common animals from this category are snakes, dragons, crocodiles, and salamanders. They represent freedom and liberation followed by transformation and adaption.

Bird Symbolism and Meanings

Are you ready to spread your wings and fly? The symbolism representing birds is a clear signal to do just that. However, there is so much more to learn from bird spirits. How does your particular spirit bird live in their natural surroundings? Are they lone birds, or do they naturally tend to flock? Do they have a loud, raucous cry, or does their birdsong speak to the soul?

Many cultures believe that birds are the natural link to higher beings, and when they are sent to visit us, it is a truly magical event. They are the harbingers of Spring, and when they come to you as a helpmate, it is a sign of transition. You may have become stuck in your routine and need a push to move on. Birds help you elevate your conscious being and soar. Because they exist in a world that lies between the Earth and the air, they represent both elements.

Other Common Meanings of Spirit Birds

• Bluebirds mean love and luck.

• Brown birds mean you need to get your health checked or you are on the road to recovery.

• White birds represent positivity and the time for change.

• Woodpeckers mean you are ready for change and they also teach the art of non-conformity.

• Swans are a symbol of purity and innocence and are often sent to people who are struggling with their romantic relationships.

• Parrots represent your voice, both in the physical world and the spiritual realm, and are sent to you to encourage you to use your words wisely.

• Owls are sent to you when it's time to be silent; they symbolize facing your shadows and overcoming your demons.

• A goose will appear in your dreams when you need protection and defense.

- Ravens are the most powerful spirit birds and are sent to guide you on the next transmutation stage of your spiritual journey.

Fish Symbolism and Meanings

Fish exist in water and are subject to rough currents and other powerful elements. They are symbolic of the subconscious emotions and periods of strife that can affect human lives. When you encounter a fish or crustacean spirit animal, it means it's time for rebirth and a deeper examination of your emotional ties.

As with the other categories, there are myriad species within the fish world, and each has a specific meaning. You can learn from them in many ways, like how they exist in nature. Are they hunters, or are they prey? Do they swim alone, or are they found in shoals?

Here are the more common members of the fish family and their spiritual meanings:

- Seahorses are the only species whose male members can fall pregnant. They represent a strong male force that can mean you need to step up as a dad or turn to your father for help.

• Salmon are well known for swimming against the tide, so they are telling you to persevere in times of trouble and keep going despite all obstacles.

• Crabs are a symbol of change and taking a new direction.

• Angelfish are the colorful and beautiful embodiment of a genuine connection to the Divine force.

• Barracudas are sent when you need strength and a quick escape from trouble.

• Sharks represent the courage to take a new path and leave your fear behind.

Insect Spirit Guides Symbolism and Meanings

Insects are the most diverse class of animals as they live everywhere. They fly, they dig, and most importantly, they pollinate everything that grows. Most people see them as an annoying part of the ecosystem, but they are actually the natural world's backbone.

The global symbolism of insects represents some of their common traits. Nurturing, productive, tenacious, and possessing a community spirit are all part of their natural makeup.

Some of the More Common Spirit Insects and What They Mean

- Spiders are one of the most creative elements in nature. They represent power and magic and being trapped in a spiritual rut.

- Wasps are the natural warriors of the insect world; they are sent to encourage you to fight for what you want.

- Scorpions are a sign your life is toxic, and you need to step away from the negative people in your environment.

- Ladybugs tell you it's time for love and teach you how to attract things you want.

- Fireflies are the shining beacon of nature and represent your time to shine; they will show you how to become better at social interactions.

- Bees produce honey, so when they appear in your dreams or as symbols, it's time for sweetness to become part of your life.

Mammal Spirit Signs, Symbolism, and Meanings

Every single day we encounter mammals in one form or another. They are our closest relatives on Earth, so it seems obvious they will be the spirit animal form that appeals to us the most. Mammal spirit animals and symbols are strongly connected to the heart of Mother Nature. They will help you attune your inner vibrations with her rhythms and cycles so you can remember the messages that come from nature.

Global symbolism of mammals includes a connection to the land, natural rhythms, physical grounding, and the need for consistency.

Some of the more common spirit mammals and what they mean:

> • Yaks are a symbol of brute strength and brawn and are sent to help you when subtlety just hasn't worked.

> • Wolves are enigmatic beings who live in packs yet can survive as lone operators; they are sent to tell you it's time to make your position known in your pack or consider breaking away and becoming self-sufficient.

> • Weasels are sent to help people with low self-esteem build their confidence.

> • Tigers help you to discover your sense of adventure and let leash your curiosity.

• Snow leopards are a symbol of peace and stillness. They are sent to tell you to take a step back and smell the roses.

• Reindeer are symbolic of a change in both career and in the physical sense. They are telling you it's okay to move far away or contemplate your current profession.

• Rabbits are a symbol telling you to look before you leap.

• Possums are a sign that danger is lying ahead, and you need to step back and let it pass.

• Orangutan spirit animals represent wisdom, and intense, fierce intelligence.

• Lions symbolize the ultimate strength and will bring you the ability to keep your family safe while releasing your inner cub when needed.

• Groundhogs are the spirits way of telling you to respect nature's cycles and get your life back on track.

• Foxes trot into your spiritual energies to tell you it's time to develop your psychic senses and abilities.

• Dolphins represent self-love and community.

• Dogs represent unconditional love and teach you to be less judgmental.

• Bears are symbolic of courage and strength.

• Anteaters symbolize the need for solitude and introspection.

Mythical Creatures Symbolism and What They Mean

How can creatures from fantasy and the mythical world have the same spiritual strength as animals from the ecosystem? Sometimes nature just doesn't cut it when we need our minds to be blown, and we need to sit up and take notice. Some of the more popular fantasy creatures are amalgams of real animals who have been imbued with supernatural powers. For instance, the Dragon has properties relating to the snake and the lizard, yet they can fly and breathe fire. The Griffin is also a compound creature made up of eagle and lion elements, carrying messages from both animals.

These archetypes of the mystical world can be relied on to drag perceptions out of the black and white reality you live in and expand your cultural wisdom.

Some of the more well-known fantasy animals' symbolism and what they mean:

• The unicorn brings you the opportunity to see the world through new eyes.

• Phoenix spirits will visit you when you need to heal; they show you how great things can emerge from even the most tragic circumstances.

• The mermaid symbolizes a balance between heart and mind; they will teach you how to achieve a healthy outlook and become a well-rounded person.

• Dragons tell you it's time to rekindle your fire and work on your soul.

• Bigfoot or any of his alter egos are a reminder to stand up to bullying and stand your ground.

While this guide will help you understand the basic meanings behind spirit guides in animal form, it is by no means comprehensive. If you find that spirit animals regularly contact you, it will help if you study ancient cultural beliefs and the connections they have with animals. The subject is a fascinating insight into spiritual interpretation and connecting with the natural phenomenon surrounding you.

Conclusion

Now you have the power to contact your spiritual guides and elicit their help; these practices will soon become part of your normal life. Just like you pick up the phone to ask your best friend what to do, you will soon be asking your guides for advice. Every experience is special and should be treated as such. So, if you are ready to welcome love and compassion into your life, go for it!

I hope you have enjoyed reading this book and have found it to be both informative and helpful. Good luck, stay safe, and embrace your spiritual team!